The
Backwaters
Press

THE BACKWATERS PRIZE IN POETRY

SKIN MEMORY

John Sibley Williams

The Backwaters Press ⭇ *An imprint of the University of Nebraska Press*

Library of Congress Control Number: 2019017151

Set in Arno Pro by A. Shahan.

Contents

✻

🜚

Acknowledgments

The author extends his heartfelt gratitude to the following journals for previously publishing poems, some in different versions, in *Skin Memory*.

American Literary Review: "Fog"
Asheville Poetry Review: "Killing Lesson"
Atlanta Review: "On Being Told: *You Must Learn to Burn Like This*"
Barrow Street: "Tonight's Synonyms for Sky"
Bluestem: "Says a Father to the Night from His Emptied Nest"
Columbia Poetry Review: "Everything Must Belong Somewhere"
Confrontation: "The Length of the Field"
Contrary: "Inventing Fire in Northern Michigan in December"
Cream City Review: "On Being Told: *White Is a Color without Hue*"
december: "After-Bruise"
Emrys Journal: "Symptoms of Shelter"
Exit 7: "Adagio" and "[this is only a test]"
The Florida Review: "Hekla (Revised)," "Nocturne," and "The Animal"
Fourteen Hills: "Then We Will Make Our Own Demons"
Hiram Poetry Review: "Rules of Common Landscape"
Jabberwock Review: "Dewpoint"
The Journal: "Snake. Tree. Rope. Wall."
Juked: "One Horse Town"
Live Encounters Poetry & Writing: "Swing"
Los Angeles Review: "Sanctum"
The Madison Review: "Forge"
The Massachusetts Review: "Closure"
Meridian: "Sons of No One"
Mid-American Review: "We Can Make a Home of It Still"
The Minnesota Review: "Star Count"
New Orleans Review: "Off Season" and "Always Greener"
New South: "Poison Oak"
North Dakota Quarterly: "St. Helens [1980]"

Poached Hare: "Skin Memory" (reprint)
Poet Lore: "Compared to Even the Smallest Star, the Moon is a Child"
Poetry City, USA: "Variations on a Theme"
Poetry Northwest: "A Brief History of a Perfect Storm"
Poetry South: "New Farmers' Almanac"
Redivider: "Death is a Work in Progress"
Salt Hill Journal: "Skin Memory"
Saranac Review: "Than the Dead," "Prelude to Again," and "Anything Can Be Made a Halo"
Sequestrum: "Outage," "Fog," "Death Is a Work in Progress," "Skin Memory," and "St. Helens [1980]"
Third Wednesday: "As a Child, Drawing Purgatory"
Trailer Park Quarterly: "Fog" (reprint)
TriQuarterly: "Father as Papercut"
Two Thirds North: "Salt Is for Curing"
Vallum Magazine: "It Was a Golden Age of Monsters"
Vinyl: "Spectral"
West Branch: "For C. D. Wright"
Whiskey Island: "As Above, So Below"
Wisconsin Review: "There Is Still"
The Worcester Review: "Absence Makes the Heart"
The Yale Review: "On Being Told: *You Must Learn to Pray*" and "On Being Told: *You Must Learn to Love the Violence*"
Yemassee: "Before, and the Birds After"
ZYZZYVA: "Natural History"

Segments from "Dear Nowhere" have been published in *Permafrost, Kentucky Review, Pilgrimage,* and *Packingtown Review.*

"Fog" appears in *Listening to Poetry: An Introduction for Readers and Writers,* edited by Jeremy Trabue (Salem OR: Chemeketa Press, 2019).

And a very special thanks to the editors and judges of the following contests:

"Fog" won the 2015 *American Literary Review* Award for Poetry and was nominated for a 2016 Pushcart Prize.

"Skin Memory" won the 2015 Philip Booth Poetry Prize from *Salt Hill Journal*.

"The Length of the Field" won the 2016 *Confrontation* Poetry Prize.

"We Can Make a Home of It Still" won *Mid-American Review*'s Fineline Competition.

"Dewpoint" won the 2016 Nancy D. Hargrove Editors' Prize from *Jabberwock Review*.

"Death Is a Work in Progress" won the inaugural *Redivider* Blurred Genre Contest.

"As a Child, Drawing Purgatory" won the 2016 *Third Wednesday* Poetry Contest.

"It Was a Golden Age of Monsters" won second place in the 2015 *Vallum* Award for Poetry.

"Before, and the Birds After" was a finalist for the 2016 *Yemassee* Poetry Prize.

SKIN MEMORY

Skin Memory

I have begun to understand that the Inupiaq language itself
is a form of resilience, that poems are a form of resilience.

    —Joan Naviyuk Kane

Because you are what song breaks open your throat and because the
same century burns a different mark into me. For now I can just listen.
To how choreographed our forgetting. To the dark little narratives of
this is mine / yours, in that order. Can you sing this country its name?

Because skin has a memory all its own and because memory is a
language that's survived its skin. For now I just walk the waist-high
replanted pines of unassimilation, carrying my words like anchors
through an open field of oars.

Snake. Tree. Rope. Wall.

When it has been night this long
we learn to see with our hands.

I know groping for names
takes the form of prayer
for some people while others
engineer new dreams from the blindness.

Not everything begins all at once
with elephant. Not everything ends
once the details decide on a context.

A thousand crows beat against night.
As we're left with only a few fallen feathers
truth is what I make of it.

For example, the sky in my hand today feels
silk-spined and smooth and spirited by the wind.
The wind feels like wherever it's come from.

Today my father is a slack line
running dead across the lake.
Let's agree to call what we're touching his hand.
Let's say it's still warm.
Let's agree our hands are enough to judge.

Let's say the hollows in his skull are
eyes and that all eyes can shine
if you sweep the flies from them.

Let's say we are certain of this one thing

then let's never touch it again.

Dewpoint

And it starts
with a moth caught in a lidless jar

or barn fire horses beating themselves
against the frame of a wide open door,

nettles and unmended cuffs, fraying,
the full force of a father's fist:

to a physicist, *causality*. Or
—let's say they're wrong—

there are no preludes, matchsticks.
The flame has always been here.

Maybe it doesn't take winter to make a tree
in winter or dewpoint to vague a morning field.

And of mothwings against glass?
A mother's tears? Those damned stupid horses

burning all night as if the earth demanded
sacrifice? The earth is silent.

The hanging rope's for hanging.
The body's dust is dust.

Hekla (Revised)

The opening to hell is the mouth of a
mountain in Iceland or anywhere,
really, remote enough to border on
the sacred. Unknowable light greens
the night sky. In time, lava hardens into
landscape, and we walk over old fires
as if history cannot burn us. If Jules
Verne had actually journeyed to the
center of the glacier the world rests
on—heavily, like a grandfather sunk
into a worn armchair dreaming of half-
healed wars—he would have known
there is no center. No past tense. No
word that means the same translated
back to its native silence. Every few
thousand years the holy betrays us: ash
darkens firmament, fire surges from a
dying culture's mouth. That nothing
dies for long is a story we tell ourselves
to make the earth easier to sing, to
convince the earth we may have once
added something to it.

St. Helens [1980]

Sometimes deer stop returning to the river to drink. Just like that. Ash lacquers the surface for a few months and over the bodies it compresses into a kind of stone. Funereal, the sky returns to those biblical days our grandparents recounted over our tightened eyes, feigning sleep. When we dreamed it was always of this. Of them, angry gods. Of constant featureless night. And still. Perhaps it's true: I haven't lost much recently, at least compared to the deer that won't be here when the water cleanses itself blue again. I'd like to say we are a patient people, a stone people, that something good will come from waiting for the sun to reemerge to lengthen our shadows.

Then We Will Make Our Own Demons

This is what happens
when no one has set the living room
ablaze in decades.

When mother calls across an empty field
and all her children come running
from the shadows, safely, home

to an abundant plate; every time,
ripe apples and merciless wholeness.
Thighs unbruised even after clenching

the belly of a mare there was no need
to break. When not a series of slaps
but the earth gently folding up upon itself

is what hardens the mountains. When father
was a mountain. And still has not proved himself
otherwise. When lumps of sugar are enough

for kids to learn the names of trees. *This
is a sycamore. Sweet, bloodless sycamore.
Son, this is how you carry moonlight*

into the house. When the bodies
flapping away, half-mast, are all cotton
and glory. Petrifying crows. Harvest.

When your name is less an arrow
pulled from whatever you felt you had
to fell; instead it is a thread dissolving

into a forgotten wound. When all wounds
have hints of birds in them. Sometimes
the whole bird. When the whole damn bird

fits in your eye, and you are nothing but love
for a candle inching closer to the sofa. *Mom,
here it is. Here is the moonlight.*

It Was a Golden Age of Monsters

The sickle moon bobs like a child's paper boat
between silhouettes of paper mountains. I am watching

steam swell off a herd of bison in a black-and-white
book about the American West. Too young to read

much into what I'm reading. The world is all image,
unfinished rail track and Douglas fir, level saw cuts, rings

tracing back to the beginning. The dozen spears projecting
from a felled paper beast are replaced the next chapter

by rifles and iron and the same falling. Tomorrow
it will snow and my father will drive me down

to the hospital again. Snowflakes crazing
about our headlights. Paper moon between

the mountains. I will be thinking about bison,
blood on the page, not the pillow. The road

that curls home always seems to erase itself.
And the steam coming off it, frail as breath.

Sons of No One

So far all the suicides have been men
    in my family. When I draw them

close, it helps to remember the lake
    beneath the desert the animals

cannot taste but know exists.
    It helps to draw them hungry

clusters of light loping across the night
    sky, such flames in their bellies. To connect

each with my finger and name
    this little universe after the gods

our god swallowed to give us
    a glimpse into creation.

Spectral

Whatever it was returns to shadowy
forest, & everything is mine, alone,
again, for the night. But I can't keep
my eyes from the near distance, out
beyond my grasp, where the world
eases calmly to nowhere. Broken by
a brief act of witness. Like a mother
glued to a monitor, as the beats still:
as she rubs her emptying belly: as a
breeze does odd things to the trees:
as if what chains them to us is more
than air.

＞

Each body is an outpost, populating,
on its way to becoming a city. How
the lights multiply, the surrounding
darknesses swell: how the moment
speaks in future tense: if I'm being
honest, how we miss what we never
quite had, holding the light up to it-
self, saying *this is what we needed you
to be.*

＞

Whatever it was we needed returns
in unrecognizable forms. The tear in
a screen door, letting winged things
loose inside. The white-tailed deer
on a field's edge, closer, so close it
dissolves in my hands. Spilled glass
of expired milk. How we can't stop
drinking it off the kitchen floor. On
all fours, as if in prayer, drinking up
the pale face, rippled, looking back.

Symptoms of Shelter

If I could reconcile the fullness
of the moon, of the black oak
tonight's moon illuminates,

with the bodies I've seen
in photographs hanging from
an oak at night in just this light.

There are only so many perfect
moments allowed us; why
must they all end with the sky

constricting, bleeding, the trees
emptying of birds. Buckshot
in the distance. Dog bark and

goodnight. Everywhere
the dead and nothing
to be done. This familiar field

now going strange.
How lucky I have been
to love, and love blindly.

Everything Must Belong Somewhere

Just past the factory where old men
silently sandpaper legs for machines
to assemble into tables, there isn't
so much a roaring sea as a graveyard
of off-cuts crackling and fast burning
into evening. The air is thick enough
to hold and be held, to make something
for us to believe in. What we make
might be called love in another language.
But we call it *absence*. We say *almost*.
Awkward hands up blouses and stolen
whiskey jars and all those notes bundled
up in the belly of an unplayed guitar.
How to sing them? To get out of the way
and let things sing through us? I think
I miss myself in them. I think my father
misses something too. Everything begins
with missing. This dance that seems all
body. Our teenage limbs windmilling
the smoke from the wood that wasn't
good enough for home. We call it home.

There Is Still

something thin to swing from madly
over the glory-faded cottonwood. A
different kind of rope & knot, sure,
& a different purpose. But our limbs
haven't changed much; all ascent &
greed. The sky yielding just enough
of itself to urge us higher. They say
there's nothing left to worship; I'd
agree if not for the dust kicked up
every slow, steady swipe we take at
erasure. What our grandfathers said
their fathers did. The haunted house
of our bodies, creaking open, almost
forgiven. Lately, the dead calm of a
summer by the lake where someone
told me someone once hung a child
for loving another child has lost its
grace. What we say to the fire in our
lungs doesn't change. Same tree. I'd
assume we throw the same shadow
long & dark over grass & stone. We
all have reasons, Mark. I hope I am
swinging to remember.

—for Mark Strand

Nocturne

No one's drowned in the boarded-up
well out back in a century. When I
pry up the nails to let in some sky,
the voices the moss maintained rise
like a cloud of bats from the mouth
of a cave. Hungry to be heard, as any
static thing, I say to the dead *you are
lucky to be so permanent, so practiced
at loneliness, so close, so goddamn close
to journey's end.* Maybe they've had
enough of this living forever. Maybe
the mystery has never been the
where or how, but why this need to
be forgotten. There are many ways
to scream so no one hears, and each
sounds just like a child alone again
in a night-heavy farmhouse, making
monsters of his shadow and friends
with his dead, running wild out into
the dark with only a hammer and his
silence; a door he can't remember
opening slamming shut behind him.

New Farmers' Almanac

Spent crops. Burnt seed.
What should have been
thin strips of walkable earth
organizing this field lit
copper by evening into paths
is now wide-open space,
pathless. At least the world
still smells like the world:
dirt-rich, deliberate,
as much oak as animal.
Rust and old oil. Blood.
Everything else is an orphanage.
New. Empty. As if everything
dies wilder than it began.
In a kitchen watching
men with my cheekbones
drag machinery over
scorched earth, someone
who is not yet me,
up on tiptoe, cranks
the hands of a clock
forward thinking
there may be some music
left inside tomorrow.

On Being Told: *You Must Learn to Burn Like This*

Cities should be seen at a distance at night at the halfway point between enter and escape. Look—how our manmade stars cluster together for warmth: archipelagos flickering in a sea of glass, fireflies burning into the distant ridgeline. I only ask to be as dangerous as a failing bridge. As a cigarette sparking refuse in a barrel, warming a dozen empty hands. I only ask to be this version of a man. But living takes its time making a fire of me. The city still looks like the sky a child holds. I don't ask to be that beautiful. I can't ask what you see in me when all the lights go out, from that middle distance of leaving and, *maybe, please,* returning.

Advice Picked Up along the Way

Sometimes it's best to kneel, stained
& sea-slick, torn, bloody as a body
can be, among the tidewrack. Some-
times it's good not to see the bottom
or know if you've made it that low.
The moon hung from a single uncut
string hoards all the light & the men
you used to look up to: mere shapes
without substance. In the gathering
distance, a river empties itself out
entirely into an insatiable sea. Some-
day you'll also learn to be satisfied
without being full. Life may not get
easier or harder or different than we
imagined, but the weight feels right
for the deeds we drag behind us. Or
the silences, sometimes heavier. Not
an anchor, son, it's best to be a whet-
stone scraped smooth by the tides;
for those wide white waves to break
briefly for your body, as if finally, son,
finally you've made an impact.

Swing

You push hard from behind. Earth
runs perpendicular beneath. My
feet strike the air in great blows
meant to ward off the gods.
Those wished-upon stars not
so unattainable, cold. I am no
longer just a body wrapped in
body wrapped in impossibilities.
Where something brutal once
hung, a plank of wood & two cuts
of rope. When we cannot conjure
metaphors of our own, we borrow,
repurpose. Thrust & trust. Sweet
sweet sway. It all feels too much like
sex for me to think of childhood. I
cannot tell which of us is entering
& which is the door we are hoping
to close.

Adagio

Please don't say you can see my father's father in my face when I cry over fireflies, dimming. This porch cannot sustain both sky and shadow. Shadows: shifted and lengthened by dawn. Ancestors: earth-swallowed, de-starred, god enough for now. Our universes hold together by strings and cups strung between men speaking softly to each other like children. Don't tell me again of the river slowly, so slowly, they crossed to get here.

Say I am a son, not just the image of a son captured by impossible light in a young mother's eyes.

Now the wind's picking up: cigar smoke and ash, tangled viscera of ivy, boys gone to men gone to relic, and back. As our hammock strings strain right up to snap. Dawn: maybe a green so green it hurts. Green: maybe the field behind someone else's home. River: this home, my father's father, crying. Tell me of this river. Now tell me of the crossing. When you call me in from playing *man* in this dimming field of men, when you call me, tonight, mother, say *firefly*.

Killing Lesson

This is the part where we crush
the most beautiful crayon in the box
beneath our bare heels
and refuse
to wash our feet.
The part of the story
where childhood falters. That palm
we cut on a stray nail.
How we spend
the rest of the summer
convincing our friends of our divinity.
When they laugh, how old we feel.
How some of us close their wounds
as others slash at their free hand
and smear themselves on everything.
We are not yet at the part
where sorrow becomes its pantomime
or blood learns to brown.
The house hasn't burned yet.
Our thumbs can still block the sun
without scar. Let's forget that time
we torched a haze of ants.
Let's call that prologue. Let's call it draft.
Pretend we can revise.
Like that stolen bicycle's plunge
into the quarry in reverse.
We are so close now to the part
where some of us eat
and the rest of us are eaten.

For C. D. Wright

For dying this way is like beginning
again. Sparrow trill waking us up to
neglected forms of light. From utter
ruin, a still image capturing the best
of us; monochrome moment handed
down generations as proof we were
here. No sanctuary. No control over
the narrative. No body beyond sea-
scape broken by one backlit figure,
deeply shadowed, verging on joy or
madness. It's so hard to tell without
the scent of sandalwood if this is
meant as eulogy or night-song. Since
when was there a contrast between
coffin and candle, an uncharted lake
and the one we spent every summer
swimming from shore to shore as if
all of humanity depended on us? All
of humanity depends on us dying
this way: poem to grief to one living
word, set against a stationary sky.

Rules of Common Landscape

There are nights we burn
couches in the old highway's
center lane until one
in a stream of long-haul trucks
lifts our little holocaust skyward
and brilliant like a Catherine wheel
of scorched cloth.

There are nights the crushed
beer cans in the dried-out
riverbed make for good
enough pillows.

And when we love
these nights with flesh
and fingernails deep within
deciduous shadow it is only
to foretaste grief.

The theory goes
we've been told the moon
is composed of so many
impossible things
we're left to pray to
whatever we can make
spark. Dammit, we can
make the world spark
for a night. I believe all
our little massacres
are held together
by Scotch tape
steadily and sadly
unsticking.

On Being Told: *You Must Learn to Pray*

For the occasional carcass
dragged skyward by crows.

All those little mouths hungering
inside our mouths. The silence

we resist in ourselves as much as
for the silence we honor in others.

Paper lanterns freed upon a calm
paper lake. Not for the lake, really,

but the way the candles balance there,
for a while. For a nearly empty hand-

ful of grandfather's thinning hair.
The wars he retreats to at night

while starlessly
coughing into a pillow.

For all ruined monoliths. Enduring
mountains gone to ruin by the earth, settling.

Watching my hands unmake what they have taken
decades to try to make beautiful.

Only beautiful; not holy.
Not sky, really; just a little closer.

Always Greener

We've made suffering a longing for a
body pierced by nails. Hung from
an x of wood high enough the world
can see us & weep. Adore // pardon.
Worship // grieve. A heaven filled
with virgins or harps or family or
nothing but silence. We miss the city
our city was built on, though no one
alive has ever lived there. We claim
the crops are failing in the height of
spring & how every year before this
one greened long & true into winter.
When we stub our toes on the mid-
night table leg, we curse the sky &
curse the pain & ask how anyone
endures until morning. It is morning
now, & we don't know which story
to burn for, which burning will hurt,
briefly, & exalt us.

Dear Nowhere

{Butte, Montana}

An aluminum bullring. Earth kicked up into a furious mist.
Evening. My hand dragging
      the sunken head of a beast toward evening, as well.
The safe word here is silence. This is when I know I've gone
just far enough. When the sun swallows the earth,
                        odds are it will be like this.

❧

{Somewhere in North Texas}

          Failing
to separate ground and sky, I'm complicit
in the steady collapse of clouds over barns.
Look—how red they rise from this dry
                  body of earth.

Is this only body placed on our tongues? Is this blood
we're washing it all down with? I'm watching
bales of hay unfasten in the distance and wondering

if in another rendering of paradise we wouldn't be
throwing stones to silence the owls at night.

❧

{Cheyenne, Wyoming}

Boy on the threshold of song. Boy swallowed
up by a flannel two sizes too large
                    and a mountain
of dust from cars returning east.
Boy made up almost entirely of stone and summer, broad
                         empty sky,
                  osprey, owl, hard brown bread. Boy
hawking horses whittled from cedar
alone beneath
a rusty tin roof with one wall

                    that from the rearview tapers off
                    to the point of never having been there at all.

                    ⤙

{Along the Inside Passage, Alaska}

How hemlock swallow the sky, for example. From a silent evening
understory, how their slight sway unsteadies the solid world.
        Though deep into summer, my hands
are bluing. The stove flame is dying. Everywhere owls emerging
from the palpable absence of eagle.

                    There is always a lake,
and here the crossing is shallow
between shore and shore. The weight of a body,
different than I remember. *Approaching darkness,* I ask,
please don't consume my body entirely, this time.

                    ⤙

{Ames, Iowa}

Husked and heaved
into the endless flat of a pickup.
Then butter and salt.
              Sustenance.
Shadows of crop dusters. The burning
scent of gasoline and what it takes
for things to remain this green.
              My grandfather
once showed me a way to castrate a bull that tradition says
causes the least suffering. I am embarrassed at how easy
flesh separates from flesh, how delicious the living
world, how I show my gratitude.

{Elsewhere in North Texas}

Screech owl. Hummingbird. Mockingbird. They say
a few red wolves remain in the outskirts of dusk.
              Be faithful
first to the heavens, then to yourself.
Third must be the world. I'm sure third is the world,
the armadillo balling up when we poke it with an oak branch.

{Duluth, Minnesota}

Pipe smoke and thin strips of flypaper.
              Citronella. Red, swollen skin.
A hesitancy of light struggles through night clouds.
And where once the stars, stories.

We are passing around our pasts like whiskey.
Then comes the whiskey. Smooth
and unquestionable myth.

      Three sizes larger than truth,
the morning's catch of walleye and salmon.
The fight still going on in the elk head above us.
Our shadows lengthening across a lawn that ends
in lake, and somewhere out there in the dark,

          past the lake, another country.

❧

{Gettysburg, Pennsylvania}

Like something too closely held to understand,

      this field. And for the first time
since my christening my father is weeping.
Is this the god people talk about at night

        when they've finished talking?

Only if they exhume every inch of bone
that fastens my great-great-great-grandfather to my femur

    will I get to ask
how much of the field is really ours.

❧

{Yellowstone National Park, Wyoming}

Bison thrum. The darkness breathes.
And spear tips flicker in the firelight.
There's bull elk implied. Or aspen sharpened by shadow.
Flame with a circle of stones to temper it.

The disembodied
words of Whitman and cormorant returning; on the wind,
my mother before I knew her, or just after. Vaguely,
in the distance, water's fall and water's crash,
the sound of everything I've failed
                    to keep safe. And home.

Tonight's Synonyms for Sky

After enough pilgrims have kissed its feet, any statue can be holy. Any estuary, even after swallowing a few children, can be known again as a place of solace. Just give it some time. If you watch the boats return empty year after year, how little it takes for a single herring or crab to grow miraculous. After a few drinks what we fear most about night takes a softer form. The thing about this sky is: whatever names we give it are as temporary as those we keep giving and erasing from ourselves. The satellites a child pulls from the outer darkness can be called stars, for a time. Any star, even if it burnt out long ago, is enough to read our dreams by. It's true: nothing much has changed since our great-great-grandfathers failed to find that gold in the dried up old riverbed on the wilder side of a wilded country. The sun that rolled around in their pans they called god, until it wasn't god so much as a conversation with their own hands. Maybe I need to give it more time. I haven't been drunk all that long, and these statues still taste too much like our lips.

Closure

Almost immaterial

          in the way of paper

animals folded fireside—   haloed and almost-
burning,   a branch of sun-lit starlings
                eclipsed by their lengthening

                        shadows.

In a matter of days, the entire forest between my window
and our town has undressed. Late afternoon shadow
escorts each leaf until earth swallows one, then the other.
All presentation removed, my ignorance of nakedness has
a chance to shine. I cannot tell chestnut from dogwood,
deer tracks from where I mark my way. The moon enters
the sky like a hole made entirely of *yes*es, in which every
no, not quite, and *once you were the world* resides.

This is the how of it: my finger carves her name from the air.

        From the shapelessness
we too were born and will return to,   a sudden
     temporary form—
              birds

        strung along a winter oak,

at once with and without any sort of resonance beyond
            my iris,
        making my smallness an enormous
                    opportunity   / burden.

                ❧

To all these darknesses that mean to me the world—
where *breakable* implies *broken, unseen* means *non-
existent, healing* when said aloud reveals nothing will
ever be the same, not quite:

To all these stories I've been asked to retell by candle-
light to paper cranes and autumn and unspooling fire,
and family:

somewhere deep inside the shell of her body, a child is
playing in these cold naked woods. Making a universe
of it. Dogwood or oak or whatever we've chosen to
call them.

To the shadows of starlings bent winterward, outside,

                ❧

no more than the sound they make

                    departing.

Prelude to Again

Seepage from the bit   peach   all over

the white cotton   dress her mother every Sunday

ironed free of   creases, imperfections,   scrubbed

in a bathtub raw   and with her daughter still

wearing it   grass from where her knees bent,

sun from where it bleached   her hair

and wherever the scent   of youth

soaked through;   from this sweet yellow stain,

this simple hunger, this *no*   *I cannot hold you*

like this,   this *thank god*   *your grandmother*

isn't here to see;   from this *love,*

someday you will know what it's like;   and finally

from someday knowing exactly what it's like.

As Above, So Below

Only his breath visible.   And a hammer,

bleach, some old car parts rusting

    into shelves where spiders are spinning

        homes for their flies. And me

            pinned beneath a workbench

learning how much I can see

                with my fists balled in my eyes.

        I see everything

          as singular sparks within a bright
          constellation:

that mosaic of tiny bird bones by the dog bowl,

his frantic tongue,   saliva sloshing over lip,

      biting down hard,   the concrete staining brown,

        my knees rising, arcing pale as moons across a torn

        and tearing sky.

Each mouthful of him suffers

        to make itself into music.

And a burnt-out bulb swaying overhead I am trying to make

          a shooting star.

Star Count

All the men here beat the bushes free
of birds for their sons to pluck from the
sky. Our dogs are too old to work these
fields. The morning is already old. But
I'm not ready to give up just yet on the
grassy light rising from beneath our
smoke and bluster. Too many stars left
to steal from a child's palm. Because
what follows is not always sequential.
Or shattered. Some days the sky just
has to fall. Some days we cannot stop
ourselves from bracing it. Imagine
the wind marching through us like an
unconquered city. I'm trying so hard
to imagine buckshot as constellations.
I don't know how many dead birds it
takes to empty the sky.

As a Child, Drawing Purgatory

Sky: an emptied womb. All the children here are grown or never were. All the birds, sung out. Sometimes I admire that nothing stays new for long. Boys pretend to be lots of things, but yesterday was the first time I feigned motherhood. Each frog mucked up from the lake I cradled between my hands, taught to speak exactly how I speak, for a moment becoming larger than I am. Sky as an empty womb, I see it now. I see you by the dark and weedy pond out back, Mom, weeping over frog song, trying to keep the world in check.

August, and I am learning secondhand smoke from not-too-distant brushfires and cigars. Porchside, as I draw the world as I'd like it to be, from the outside looking in, my family talking around me like magpies: constant, staccato, deaf to what the world hears when it hears us. *If* is a question too abstract for such endless summer twilight. They say *when*, as in *when* the cancer takes her and *when* the fires eventually burn cold. When I grow up they say I'll resemble my grandfather, who always looked to me like a tattered scarecrow, like a cracked leather belt so worn it feels like skin against me.

We have been here before, at least in gesture. Stars thrown around the sky, like toys I've left scattered across the living room for people bigger than me to trip over. Fruit bats complain from the vague upward darkness, and an oak tree that's seen wars begin and end around it sawed down to stump for winter fire. There is a bright white light inside I need to get out of my system. I need to break deeper than bone, take the stairs in twos and threes, swim farther from the pond's edge than I can safely return. And sometimes I need to kill something. Sometimes anything is better than waiting in waning heat for the cold to return with its smaller, controlled fires. In six months, when we thaw, the porch and smoke and uncertain highway will be like unopened buds, memories like tractors kicking up chaff and blackbirds. And I am tired of waiting. I am tired of waiting to be that scarecrow.

Off Season

Blood spills across the snow like lit
kerosene. The sun in the snow half
blinding & true as glass looked into
too long. Hobbled prints wind along
an iced-over riverbed into the forest
where the things that go to die don't
die by our hands. We'll follow what
we failed to kill all our lives.

Variations on a Theme

Say horse.
Say the fencing has rusted to bits and we are tracking

an escaped horse deep into night.
　　　Again. Desperate,
as if a single star loosened
from Orion's belt and we didn't know
　　　　　what to call it anymore.

Say home.
Say we are trying to name what we've built to complete it.

Say every nail is essential.
Every acorn. Ghost. How things lose their shape

more when lost than buried and forgotten.
　　　　　Or burned. Say this with me:

　❧

we all want things.
　　I, for example, want what I've lost

to have burned me.
　　　　Isn't that how grace works?

　❧

Say there was a girl once
or the girl still beside me
has wandered from touch.
              I'm not so sure

we're not horses, she might be saying,
as I gather her nakedness inside me
in hopes of completion.

Say love,
        how we round our empty mouths to say it.

              ❧

You know the story: it is night

where everything is retrievable

              ❧

though no one knows what is missing.

Fog

and the cranes resting over unfinished houses
and the houses, the lights left on in them, the river, all
drift off like the signature completing a suicide note.

> *~~Dear~~*
> *~~those who will love me more in my absence,~~*
>
> *Dear you who will forget what I looked like,*
>
> *~~Last night I was a drawbridge,~~*
>
> *~~Last night I was the fog swallowing a drawbridge~~*
>
> *For the first time, this morning I could see you*
> *through the fog as a drawbridge sees the ship*
> *that breaks it in two.*

Into the silence, jackhammers and invisible grinding.
Voices within voices. Even without light I know dawn
is running through the city and the larger city beneath it.

> *If destruction hinges on what is beautiful*
> *in making, let ~~my soul~~ my body collapse*
> *into ~~roots~~ something foundational.*

Now that I'm awake, it's time to carve up the day
into hour and progress. Into dig and follow. It doesn't matter
that I can't see what I know to be there.

> *Only after the body is gone do words come freely.*
> *I am sorry and you are sorry and ~~I think~~ I love*
> *that we don't know what for.*

It's as if through cloudy glass three stories above the rooftops
the sky and city alloy. Ghost ships pass through the cathedrals.
Skyscrapers bellow for the bridge to part.
There are still things that need

    to be said.

Death Is a Work in Progress

My mother says *fox* while gesturing toward an old red wagon abandoned in our yard for decades. A word so cavernous her entire body vanishes into it. Body of misfiring electrons. Scattered images, contexts. Body that is mainly just body now. No other animal knows how to be this incomplete. I think: if you were a fox, coyotes would have eaten you by now. I say: *yes, I'll climb into that fox and let you pull me through the high grass one more time.*

Poison Oak

I wanted to say something about the tingling
spreading heartward from the part of my bare
leg that brushed against the wild brush.
It could be a cautionary tale. Ancient and all
metaphor. About remaining close to home
or the dangers of scratching what needs
to be scratched. It could be
ad copy for calamine. I don't know.
I do know there's a crying boy
the coarse cradle of my hands
cannot rock into immunity.
He is a landscape of reddening splotches.
It could be he is preparing for the world.
Or preparing to leave it. Or me. Listen,
little one: even the forest shivers a little
when the wind loosens its leaves.
We could be all falling. So sleep. Dream.
And in dreaming forget I have no idea
what I'm saying when I say *I've got you.*

The Animal

All the cruelties are different, but
there's something oddly familiar
in carrying our children safely
through the world by our teeth.
In pressing an empty mouth up to
the only part of us that nourishes.
Sometimes, with winter at its
deadest, in eating our young and
starting over again in spring. It's
spring, thank god, and all we have
is an open pasture of half-broken
foals. A rusty cage for the chronic
wild. A spindle-legged wire fence
wrapped in teeth separating one
neighbor from the next. When
it comes down to it, son, I don't
think I'll ever eat you. But here I
am, telling you things you already
know about love.

Compared to Even the Smallest Star, the Moon Is a Child

One pinprick of light at a time
consumes and is consumed by
itself, like the crabgrass over
a burnt-out barn or synapses
when the forgetting takes hold.
These stars I've hooked to the
ceiling will have to do. This
empty birdcage of a mouth
we both speak from, nowadays.
This push and pull of *we*
where each of us, alone, resides.
A glass of milk, boiled and frothed
and wrapped in a cloth, cools
by the bedside. Nobody is
reaching far enough to touch.
If I stroke the recess between
your shoulder blades, saying
angel bones, what will have
changed? Or if I erase you
from the room, or never leave it?
A basin of bison merge with mist
in the painting I use to approximate
a window. Cornflower blue and
speckled with graves, the real
moon is a bedroom door, closing.

On Being Told: *White Is a Color without Hue*

The contrast between a cloud's white and the white of my teeth before sinking into meat is a matter of palettes. A matter of mercy. Beyond the upslope a mountain forms through the fog. The cap is white. And the warm milk on my bedside. Dove white. Maggot white. And the bones on my plate. The blurry edges of stars. Trailing off white. No winter is forever white. And the ones that are. It's a matter of mercy, really. Wedding white. Ghost wrapped in sheet white. As contrasted against the white of a sheet merely ghosted on a clothesline by the wind. Against the whiteness of a sheet pulled back from a face that must be identified. And the face beneath.

Salt Is for Curing

To feel the bottom:
        sand & stone. Silt. Sea snails.

What makes up the foreign world
        clumps between my toes.

Uproots. Assimilates.
        Distances collapse: now

we are merely the naming
        vs. the named, hands

vs. being held, the forsaken
        & reinhabited.

—:as a cypress collecting kites.
        —:as a child reaching up

from the crook of its branches
        toward string & color.

Salt & wound, I am standing
        knee-deep in this shipbroken

blue, as the horizon rushes in,
        coughing up shells I can slip

my entire body into
        like a coffin.

Than the Dead

The living are colder, long Montana
winter whiter; this idle light filtered
through hardy pine still more honest
than the thousand candles we've lit
to remind the world that we're here.
& the headstones in the high grass.
Those little white crosses, the huge
stone angels weeping single tears. I
don't know what to say to our kids
when they ask what happens to stars
at dawn or why we fall in love with
what we cannot see. Someone has
spilled the moon all down our night-
black walls. Someone throws water
on our long-smothered flames. Once
there was, & as suddenly no longer,
in some ways leaving the dead more
fitted to these grief-wasted nights.
Our mouths are waiting to be filled with
silence, I finally reply, though the kids
have grown up & moved on to salting
their own wounds.

Inventing Fire in Northern Michigan in December

If rubbing two sticks together would
suffice, or clashing stone into stone
until the spark opens up into a flame
bitter enough to warm us. If only we
knew how to touch ourselves in that
way that drives winter from bone, at
least how to touch each other. & if
there really is a hinge at the far edge
of night to grease & open & step in-
to morning. If all it takes is belief to
see it. Belief & blood. We'd spill it;
we've spent centuries spilling it; we
have spent centuries spilling greater
fires across far greater cities until all
that remained were ember & fable,
sometimes not even that. But here
we are, breathing our hands slowly
back to life as if we've never known
the origins of our burning, as if no
one has ever been so cold. A rusty
tin bucket we've filled with rubbish.
A steeple of kindling, like the way
our fathers showed us. The dead all
around, talking themselves hoarse.
& the sun, hidden overhead, streams
through into dawn, despite us.

One Horse Town

                    and so what
        if—disowned—this hometown

        named after some other town &
        spidered by streets named for

        trees you've never seen

        sounds like fire, now. like

        flint spark plume. smother. escape. trying
        to erase your name from the too narrow
        one-lane entrance with your heel.
                                severed—

        you've repeated to the morning
        mirror—the thread. the past. the apples
        that gripped your baby teeth, still
        raining down.

        in the garage, upside-down,
        your old bicycle, wheels spinning along
                                an open road of air.

everything but your bones
a trespass. and your bones, too.
the map in your palm. and the flame.

and that one missing shingle,
all the unpainted interiors,

and the bones interred
a week before your return

and, finally, your return.

the rain, and moving through
the rain that same horse

you named after a king
who saw home even in
the farthest edges of the world

nuzzles up to the earthen mound

as if smelling you in it.

Absence Makes the Heart

My son has not yet found a reason to
love or hate the silence following
us around the house. All he knows:
something palpable is missing, not yet
profound, not yet painting nightmares
over his sleep, just a steady lack of arms
where arms should be. The hundred
nightingales trapped in my chest are
chattering all at once. I don't know
which to speak from, if any voice is
true, & if I'd recognize it. My face tries
to shift confidently among the faces he
expects to see over his cradle at night. I
press his ear to the floorboards' groans
& say *this is the house settling beneath
us.* I say *memory is simply an attempt to
record what matters.* Then I say *nothing
really matters anymore.* & the birds
hush. & the house. & he is finding his
reason; I hope it's love, & I hate that I
have loved so much.

We Can Make a Home of It Still

Of the three-legged foal shot before mother could abandon it. Of the wolf lapping rainwater from the bowl of a dead wolf's pelvis. Timbered mountains slope into timbered hillocks. Into valleys. Unmoving steel roosters straddle wind-spun homes. We don't talk of the landscape we're born into, onto; this territory mapped on dried horsehide. We unroll it gently over earth to read the earth by. Rocks weigh down the edges so our oceans don't collide.

From the covered bridge hang two unpaired sneakers and shreds of rope from older times. We only talk about ghosts when they're nowhere in sight. The planks beneath us breathe out dust, and when we've reached the other side how quickly dust settles. Quickly and silently, everything settles back. *Just enough rope left to hang a cat by.* Isn't that what they say? When a cherry tomato bleeds all down my daughter's pale chin, she tends to laugh. I laugh at the contrast. I know all this means something.

A clothesline is only tense until it snaps. Those maples she says have all the lights of heaven inside grow monstrous at night. When they built a new railroad six miles south of town, the brakemen took to whiskey and the pews came alive, the gods a bit darker than I remember from childhood. Everything has a breaking point built into its architecture. I tell her it's not so bad wearing wet clothes to school sometimes. You'll get used to the cold cling. It's not so bad getting used to things. Like the silence of old steel tracks or the wolves that have always been here inching closer. Like the luminous trees out back with beasts living in them.

On Being Told: *You Must Learn to Love the Violence*

Like a man who sets himself on fire
on purpose every night without quite
achieving ash. This is something like
saying every stain, every scar makes
a home on the surface of a body
it can't penetrate. Why can't I mainly be
a body sturdied by love? Though sometimes,
when I feel the city dreaming itself innocent
around me again, it's true I want to liberate
the steel-springed horses from the park where my
son has learned to take and do his harm
and see how much wild is really left us. Sometimes
I want to be recognized for what I'm not,
yet. I want to show I burn, and burn bright
as the gods we're meant to fashion ourselves from.
Bright as rage, as goodbye, as a throat
unzipped to give the bullets their voice. If finally
this voice becomes the sound a man makes. Something like
the sound a man is supposed to make.

Father as Papercut

or wet leaves weighing down a barn
roof. As jagged sunrise softened by
a few itinerant clouds; the whole of
winter winnowed down to one hard
lake face. Tanned rawhide stretched
along a living room floor; forgetting
for a moment the no-longer-animal
of it. As all that peaceful space
between open palm & its clenching.
How I want to remember you: bent
metal that could be used to mark my
inner thigh or the pages of a favorite
book. As the profound resonance of
a church bell, rusting soundless.

Says a Father to the Night from His Emptied Nest

What it's like to pitch half-drunk
bottles at the dimming stars,
ruin against ruin, all the season's

hay into a meadow-sized bundle
for burning. The horses and
the children are dead or moving on.

It's up to me to trample the field
alone, to suicide by living here
thirty more years, to craft an image

of a barn to outlast these cinders.
Some say the first body, made of dust,
wept from its impotence over the world

risen from its ribs. Some say there are still
snakes under the porch speaking to us.
Once I saw a carnage of blackbirds

pecking straw from the head of a scarecrow
wearing my shirt, and for a moment I saw myself
again, beautiful in them.

Outage

Around the snapped cable line, energy wastes into the tall grass. Into our footprints filled with rain. Into the little animals living off the grass and rain, now crisp and steaming. Half the town's gone to darkness and with nothing else to do we are relearning our hands, one finger at a time. *This one goes to market. This one flees toward home. Wee wee!* I tell him, *don't worry, son, when the light returns all these little piggies will be just where we left them.* As before us a thick snake leaps and sparks. As all the dead animals dissolve into night. As night is dissolved by our candles. As I squeeze his head firmly to my chest. Until only the lie belongs to me.

A Brief History of a Perfect Storm

—Massachusetts, 1991

Our apple tree shakes loose its last
fruits & bends, nightmared, over my
boarded-up bedroom window. Dry,
swirled palette of sky Monets over-
head. Everything not nailed down
is dancing midair, weightless, like
the silence after a mother's eulogy.
If there's one thing the televised
war has failed to teach me, that I
am learning now, it's the crisp, clean
sound of a body, splitting.

The Length of the Field

Like the switch that steers a train
    down a spur that ends in grass, her legs

straddle the loose stones of a wall separating
    battlefields. Even the goneness

of musket smoke ever-present. Even bodies
    related by blood: divided, unmarked &

overrun by meadow. Horses, mostly broken.
    Her hands so small inside

each other. The dead so small. Rusted-out cannons
    & so many people nearby playing at war.

There are things never meant to last
    this long. Like wounds & flags.

My sister who was born with a river
    in her skull & these never-ending latitudes

of white ash and hickory. I keep coming back to
    the translucent flesh of her legs

splayed over stone: papery, impossible, still here
    with us. Like the hollow bones of a baby

bird; an old smoke rising from this peaceful
    lit-up acreage.

Natural History

The missing hind legs of whales. The
dried deer pelt stretched thinly over
the wall over our son's sleep. The slow
pulse oaks bring to forests before the
air thickens with smoke. The ten-
ton statue of a man riding a horse
shedding its shadow long over an
empty paddock. The herring that gave
birth to a great city. The overfished
herring that gutted this once great city,
abdomen to gill. The way men here
cry when the sky they pray to refuses
to rain. The rain and sometimes a
prayer for drought. The bowl of keys
in the foyer that open other people's
doors. The open door of a body when
the bullet exits cleanly. The shrapnel
seeing leaves behind in things. The
knowing the names of. The being
named. The gypsy moth coaxed
closer to flame. Tailbone, appendix,
vestigial wings. All we must shed
before returning to the sea.

Anything Can Be Made a Halo

Liver wrapped in butcher's paper,
               heart in muslin,
inedible flesh fed to the fire with the moon
               —not full, almost nothing,
but still visible enough tonight to halo
               the blades—our only light.

Otherwise everything is sage grass
               soaking up our stains;
horsewhip, handwork, wound,
               and wanting more of the same.

If hunger is who we are.

If who we are is seeing clearly
               —with our hands at, or so I hope,
their bloodiest—the world
               as it would like to be seen; whipped,
worked, wounded, without insisting
               on mercy.

As if mercy were the same as forgiveness,
               need synonymous with nights
out in a field taking things apart without
               learning how they work;
as if instinct, hunger; as if who we are is
               fire, and what's left

once the fire burns itself out.

After-Bruise

So, hang from the rope still strung over the sweetgum
limb a folded paper dove, a dry red tourniquet, a note
of apology. Never mind today the children filling
the tire's hollow—fearlessly swinging, bare-toeing
the clouds—are no less vulnerable. No less sacred,
and temporary. Never mind the usual body-splay of
shadow—beneath which, nothing. Just some grass.
What we've compromised in civilizing the rebel dead.

As if to say, *how does the pain we protect differ from
the break we must heal?* As if, each time differently,
hopefully, *we are finally emerging from the wrong side of
our nature.* So—you rough bark made entirely of knots,
holding our children, holding up whatever once held
the sky—fray and snap. Snap cleanly.

Sanctum

What they've died in made sacred
while what killed them is forgotten
or forgiven. No wonder history is
often pictured as a sky-bearing
cross or a sharp cut of moon or an
endless sea of candles in a guilt-
darkened room. The story as some
know it ends with tangled rebar. A
shattered school. Empty promises
made over a rich and distant earth.
I'm more familiar with young men
moving stones from caves and
waiting for their fathers to call
them home. It's a ramshackle river
we pretend to try to cross to see
ourselves beautiful on the other
shore. We are convinced we cannot
be beautiful here. We find the signs
we're looking for, and they mean
exactly what we knew they would.
I'm looking for the world the world
doesn't like to talk about above a
whisper. Some sort of unforbidden
city. A beveled hilltop overlooking
an impossible meadow made
weightless by the dead. The dead
here are so heavy. We may never
be this beautiful again.

Before, and the Birds After

This was before the children
in their classroom singing
of love and country, chained
together, hand in hand, fell
to their knees as the unrung
bell of rifle fire began in that
sudden way of bells to loosen
and clang. Before idea turned
to gesture. Before lying awake
practicing eulogies that have no
echo beyond themselves.
This was before the moon
lying closer to me than your
body turned steadily toward
the door. Two back-to-back
doors opening away from
each other. Before tomorrow
uncoupled from today. Like
something meant only after
saying it, the absence of
birds on the sycamore have
never felt more like birds, never
crashed into the window so hard
before singing.

[this is only a test]

Otherwise, everything is acre upon acre of locusts leveling the new season's prairie grass. And the fires set to drive them away. Garbled through an old radio transmitting the world through tin foil, *stay inside unless you're in the burning path*. Otherwise, I guess, we should flee in whatever direction is opposite destruction.

Children shrink under school desks and on the top floor of a swaying building I'm asked if I believe in god. There's too much desperation squeezed beneath doorframes, too many windows opening and minds set on flight. Beneath us the earth moves in predictable ways. A weeklong sandstorm in Nigeria. A young girl gathering flies at a checkpoint somewhere, still cradling a visa and sack of rice, feeding the grass. Otherwise, I'm pretty sure, everything within us says something beautiful.

Forge

—for Carl Phillips

And I saw that how we weather it will not save or deface us.
Brokenness in tow or all our parts hammered back together
and left beside the fire to cool. *We are here; this happened*: a
simple record. If we're lucky, a catalyst. One door framed
within another. Even if closure is a construct, I cannot rule out
heaven entirely. Whatever finally breaks me, I cannot refuse it.

BACKWATERS PRIZE IN POETRY WINNERS

2018 John Sibley Williams, *Skin Memory*
2017 Benjamín Naka-Hasebe Kingsley, *Not Your Mama's Melting Pot*
2016 Mary Jo Thompson, *Stunt Heart*
2015 Kim Garcia, DRONE
2014 Katharine Whitcomb, *The Daughter's Almanac*
2013 Zeina Hashem Beck, *To Live in Autumn*
2012 Susan Elbe, *The Map of What Happened*
2004 Aaron Anstett, *No Accident*
2003 Michelle Gillett, *Blinding the Goldfinches*
2002 Ginny MacKenzie, *Skipstone*
2001 Susan Firer, *The Laugh We Make When We Fall*
2000 David Staudt, *The Gifts and the Thefts*
1999 Sally Allen McNall, *Rescue*
1998 Kevin Griffith, *Paradise Refunded*

The Backwaters Prize in Poetry was suspended from 2005 to 2011.
To order or obtain more information on these or other
University of Nebraska Press titles, visit nebraskapress.unl.edu.

Lightning Source UK Ltd.
Milton Keynes UK
UKHW012359171019
351767UK00011B/130/P